SCIENCE BEHIND THE COLORS
RAINBOW BOAS

by Alicia Z. Klepeis

Ideas for Parents and Teachers

Pogo Books let children practice reading informational text while introducing them to nonfiction features such as headings, labels, sidebars, maps, and diagrams, as well as a table of contents, glossary, and index.

Carefully leveled text with a strong photo match offers early fluent readers the support they need to succeed.

Before Reading
- "Walk" through the book and point out the various nonfiction features. Ask the student what purpose each feature serves.
- Look at the glossary together. Read and discuss the words.

Read the Book
- Have the child read the book independently.
- Invite him or her to list questions that arise from reading.

After Reading
- Discuss the child's questions. Talk about how he or she might find answers to those questions.
- Prompt the child to think more. Ask: Did you know about rainbow boas before reading this book? What more would you like to learn about them?

Pogo Books are published by Jump!
5357 Penn Avenue South
Minneapolis, MN 55419
www.jumplibrary.com

Copyright © 2022 Jump! International copyright reserved in all countries. No part of this book may be reproduced in any form without written permission from the publisher.

Library of Congress Cataloging-in-Publication Data

Names: Klepeis, Alicia, 1971- author.
Title: Rainbow boas / by Alicia Z. Klepeis.
Description: Minneapolis: Jump!, Inc., [2022]
Series: Science behind the colors | Includes index.
Audience: Ages 7-10
Identifiers: LCCN 2021039026 (print)
LCCN 2021039027 (ebook)
ISBN 9781636903859 (hardcover)
ISBN 9781636903866 (paperback)
ISBN 9781636903873 (ebook)
Subjects: LCSH: Rainbow boa—Juvenile literature.
Classification: LCC QL666.O63 K55 2022 (print)
LCC QL666.O63 (ebook) | DDC 597.96/7–dc23
LC record available at https://lccn.loc.gov/2021039026
LC ebook record available at
https://lccn.loc.gov/2021039027

Editor: Eliza Leahy
Designer: Emma Bersie

Photo Credits: Michael D. Kern/NaturePL/SuperStock, cover; Pete Oxford/Minden Pictures/SuperStock, 1, 16-17; cynoclub/Shutterstock, 3; fivespots/Shutterstock, 4; Thomas Marent/Minden Pictures/SuperStock, 5; Gustavo Frazao/Shutterstock, 6-7; Michael & Patricia Fogden/Minden Pictures/SuperStock, 8-9; Murilo Mazzo/Shutterstock, 10; Alamy, 11; Ian Watt/Alamy, 12-13; Nature Picture Library/Alamy, 14-15; Geoff Trinderan/Pantheon/SuperStock, 18; Alberto Rozzoni/Shutterstock, 19; Guillermo Ossa/Shutterstock, 20-21; reptiles4all/Shutterstock, 23.

Printed in the United States of America at Corporate Graphics in North Mankato, Minnesota.

TABLE OF CONTENTS

CHAPTER 1
Rainbow on the Move 4

CHAPTER 2
Color Changers 10

CHAPTER 3
A Colorful Life 18

ACTIVITIES & TOOLS
Try This! 22
Glossary 23
Index 24
To Learn More 24

CHAPTER 1

RAINBOW ON THE MOVE

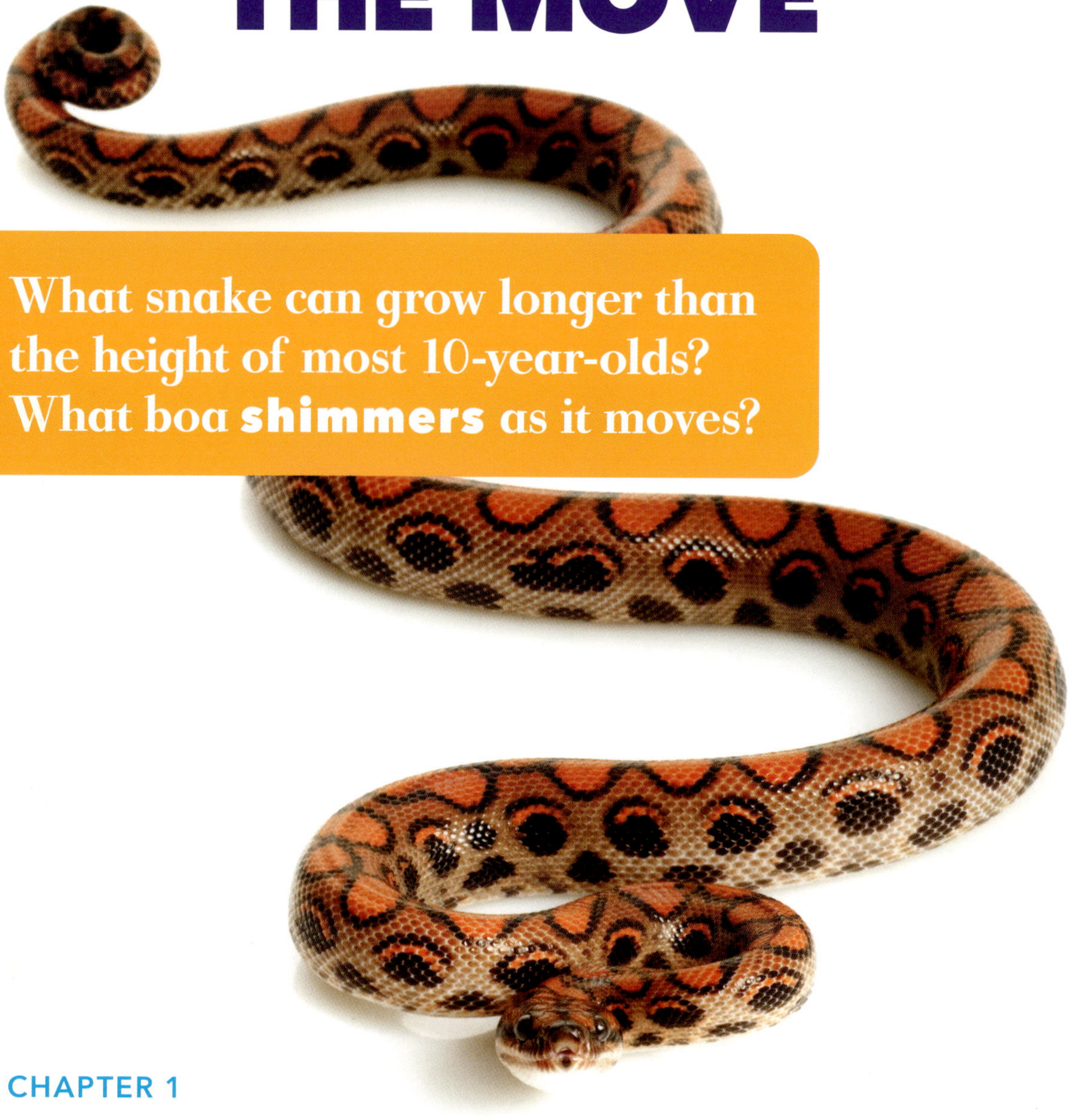

What snake can grow longer than the height of most 10-year-olds? What boa **shimmers** as it moves?

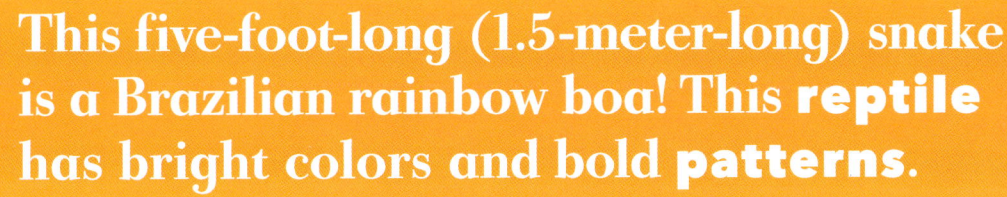
This five-foot-long (1.5-meter-long) snake is a Brazilian rainbow boa! This **reptile** has bright colors and bold **patterns**.

CHAPTER 1

The Brazilian rainbow boa is just one rainbow boa **species**. It is the most well-known. These snakes live in the Amazon basin and northern South America. They often live in rain forests.

CHAPTER 1

Their **scales** blend in with the forest floor. This **camouflage** helps them sneak up on **prey**. Rainbow boas are **carnivores**. They hunt at night. They eat birds, mice, lizards, and frogs.

Rainbow boas are great swimmers. But they don't usually hunt in the water. They often hunt along the shore or climb trees to find food.

DID YOU KNOW?

To eat, rainbow boas tightly squeeze their prey. Then they swallow it whole.

8 CHAPTER 1

CHAPTER 1

CHAPTER 2
COLOR CHANGERS

Rainbow boas are reddish brown. They have black rings on their backs. They have three black stripes on their heads.

ring

stripe

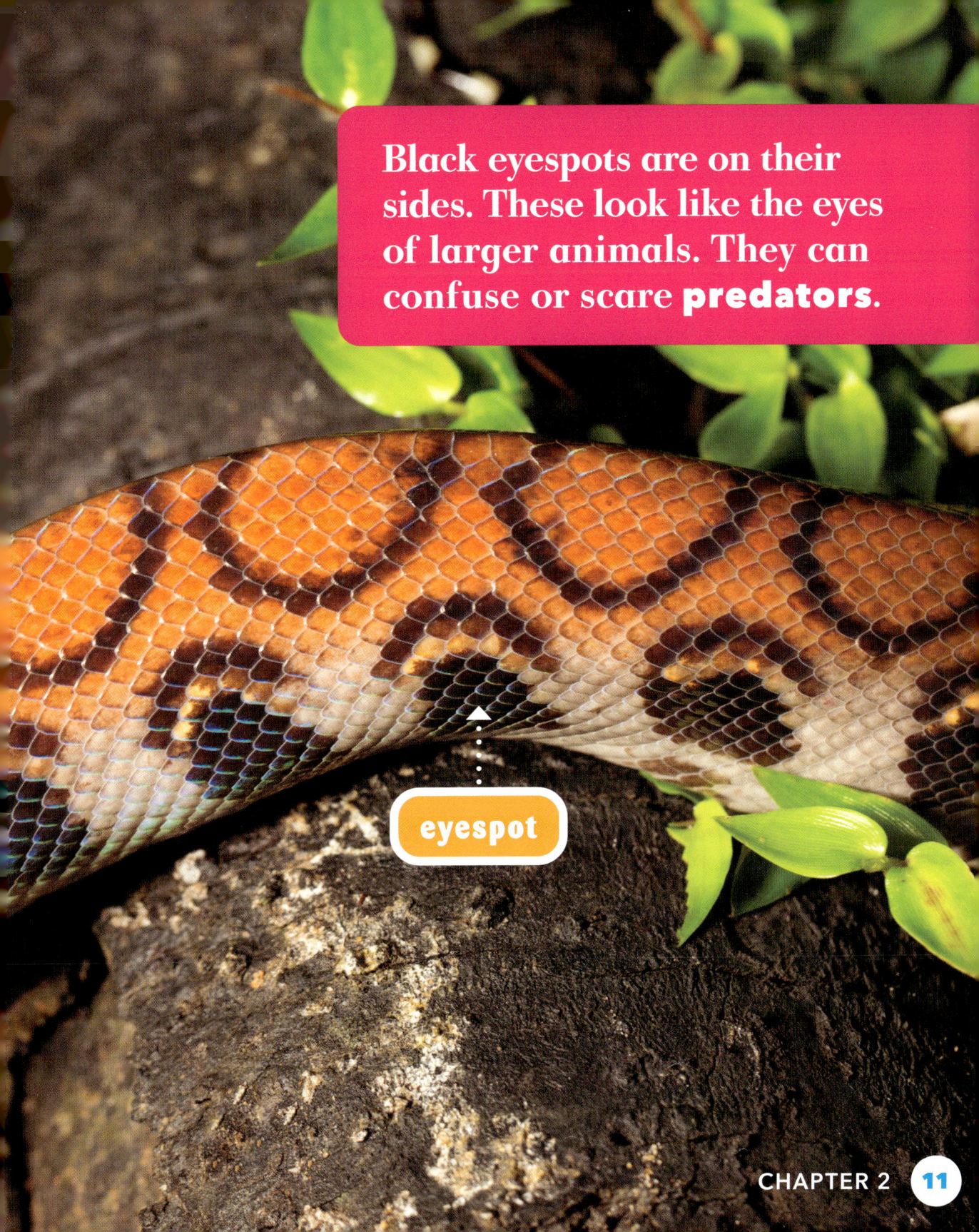

Black eyespots are on their sides. These look like the eyes of larger animals. They can confuse or scare **predators**.

eyespot

CHAPTER 2 11

When rainbow boas move, their skin shimmers. Why? Their scales act like **prisms**. When light hits them, it creates a rainbow **sheen**. The scales look green, blue, purple, yellow, and red!

12 CHAPTER 2

CHAPTER 2

A rainbow boa has two layers of skin. The top layer is the epidermis. It has scales. The bottom layer is the dermis. It has special **cells**. Some **reflect** light. Others **absorb** it. This changes the way the snake looks. It can confuse predators.

scale

TAKE A LOOK!

A rainbow boa's skin has two layers. Take a look!

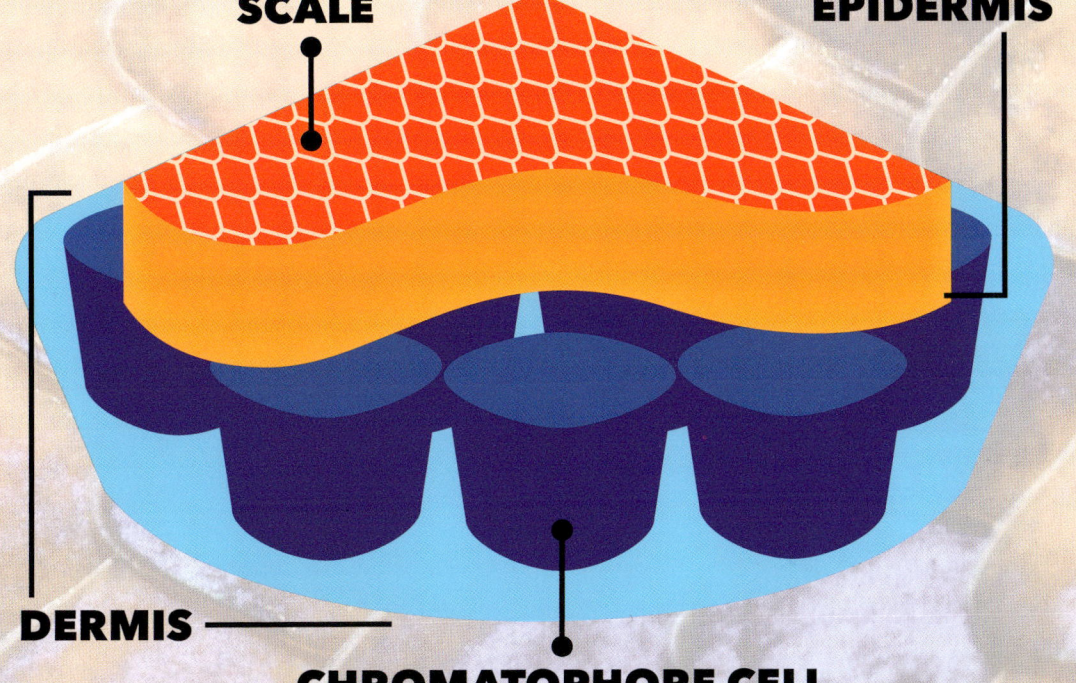

As it grows, a rainbow boa grows new skin. The new layer of skin forms under the old one. Fluid fills the space between them. It separates the old and new skin. The fluid makes the snake look cloudy. Then the snake **sheds** the skin that doesn't fit anymore. The top layer peels off.

DID YOU KNOW?

Snake skin often sheds in one long piece!

CHAPTER 2   17

CHAPTER 3
A COLORFUL LIFE

Many snakes hatch from eggs. But not rainbow boas. They are born live. These snakes are colorful from the start. Their **genes** give them their colors and patterns.

Rainbow boas develop more black coloring as they age. The rainbow sheen shows up better on adults with darker patterns.

CHAPTER 3   19

From birth, rainbow boas are colorful. Throughout their lives, their patterns and rainbow sheen help them hunt and hide. Would you like to see one?

DID YOU KNOW?

Rainbow boas are 15 to 20 inches (38 to 51 centimeters) long when they are born. That's almost as long as most human babies!